THE ULTIMATE
LAS VEGAS RAIDERS
TRIVIA BOOK

A Collection of Amazing Trivia Quizzes
and Fun Facts for Die-Hard Raiders Fans!

Ray Walker

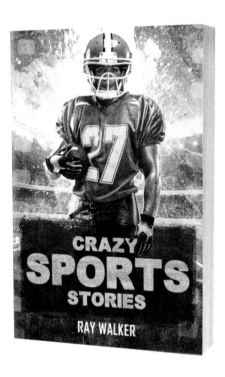

CONTENTS

INTRODUCTION

The Las Vegas Raiders were established as an American Football League team in 1960 in Oakland, California. The Raiders have consistently proven themselves to be a team that fights hard and is a force to be reckoned with in the NFL.

They won three Super Bowl championships, in 1976, 1980, and 1983 and they have won four AFC Conference championships and 12 AFC West Division championships. They are very often a threat in the AFC West, having last won it in 2002. They have made 19 NFL playoff appearances. Their most recent Super Bowl appearance was in 2002.

The Raiders have called a few different cities home, including Oakland, Los Angeles, and now Las Vegas. This has proven one thing for sure: Raider Nation is consistent across the West and will support the Silver and Black no matter where they are.

The thing about football is that it is a lot like life. There are good times and bad times, good days, and bad days, but you have to do your absolute best never to give up. The Las Vegas Raiders have proven that they refuse to give up and that they will do anything they need to do to bring a championship to the state of Nevada. Winning is more than possible when you have a storied past as the Raiders do. They have so much captivating history and so many undeniable player legacies to be profoundly proud of.

The Raiders' current home is Allegiant Stadium, which opened in 2020. They play in one of the most difficult divisions in the NFL, the AFC West, alongside the Denver Broncos, Los Angeles Chargers, and Kansas City Chiefs.

With such a rich past that goes back generations, you're probably already very knowledgeable as the die-hard member of Raider Nation that you are. Let's test that knowledge to see if you truly are the World's Biggest Raiders Fan.

CHAPTER 1:

ORIGINS & HISTORY

QUIZ TIME!

1. Which of the following cities have the Raiders never called home?

    a. Oakland

    b. Kansas City

    c. Las Vegas

    d. Los Angeles

2. In what year was the Raiders franchise established?

    a. 1958

    b. 1959

    c. 1960

    d. 1961

3. The Raiders' current home is Allegiant Stadium.

    a. True

    b. False

4. In which division do the Las Vegas Raiders play?

   a. NFC West
   b. AFC West
   c. NFC North
   d. AFC North

5. The Las Vegas Raiders were a member of the NFC West Division from 1960-2001.

   a. True
   b. False

6. How many AFC Conference championships have the Raiders won (as of the end of the 2019 season)?

   a. 2
   b. 3
   c. 4
   d. 7

7. What is the name of the Raiders' mascot?

   a. Raider Russell
   b. Red Raider
   c. Rick Raider
   d. Raider Rusher

8. Who is the winningest head coach in franchise history (as of 2020 season)?

   a. John Madden
   b. Jon Gruden
   c. Al Davis
   d. Art Shell

9. What are the Las Vegas Raiders fans often referred to as?

    a. 12th Man
    b. Raiderettes
    c. Raider Rockers
    d. Raider Nation

10. Who was the first head coach of the Raiders?

    a. Al Davis
    b. Eddie Erdelatz
    c. Marty Feldman
    d. Tom Flores

11. The Raiders franchise was originally established in Oakland, California.

    a. True
    b. False

12. What is the name of the Raiders' fight song?

    a. The Las Vegas Wind
    b. The Raider Wind
    c. The Autumn Wind
    d. The Pirate Wind

13. How many appearances have the Raiders made in the NFL playoffs (as of the end of the 2019 season)?

    a. 9
    b. 11
    c. 15
    d. 19

14. How many Super Bowls have the Raiders won (as of the end of the 2019 season)?

    a. 0
    b. 1
    c. 2
    d. 3

15. Al Davis owned the Raiders from 1972 until he died in 2011.

    a. True
    b. False

16. Which stadium was the first home stadium of the Raiders?

    a. Candlestick Park
    b. Kezar Stadium
    c. Oakland Coliseum
    d. Los Angeles Memorial Coliseum

17. How many AFC West Division titles have the Raiders won (as of the end of the 2019 season)?

    a. 9
    b. 10
    c. 12
    d. 15

18. Who is the current head coach of the Las Vegas Raiders?

    a. Mike Shanahan
    b. Jack Del Rio
    c. John Madden
    d. Jon Gruden

19. Derek Carr is the current quarterback of the Las Vegas Raiders (as of the 2020 season).

    a. True
    b. False

20. The Oakland Raiders were originally going to be called the "Oakland Señors."

    a. True
    b. False

QUIZ ANSWERS

1. B – Kansas City

2. C – 1960

3. True

4. B – AFC West

5. B – False

6. C – 4

7. D – Raider Rusher

8. A – John Madden

9. D – Raider Nation

10. B – Eddie Erdelatz

11. A – True

12. C – The Autumn Wind

13. D – 19

14. D – 3

15. A – True

16. B – Kezar Stadium

17. C – 12

18. D – Jon Gruden

19. A – True

20. A – True

DID YOU KNOW?

1. The Raiders franchise has had 20 head coaches so far: Eddie Erdelatz, Marty Feldman, Red Conkright, Al Davis, John Rauch, John Madden, Tom Flores, Mike Shanahan, Art Shell, Mike White, Joe Bugel, Jon Gruden, Bill Callahan, Norv Turner, Lane Kiffin, Tom Cable, Hue Jackson, Dennis Allen, Tony Sparano, and Jack Del Rio.

2. The Raiders' current head coach is Jon Gruden. He had previously been the head coach of the Raiders from 1998 through 2001 and of the Tampa Bay Buccaneers from 2002 through 2008. At age 39, Gruden was then the youngest head coach to win the Super Bowl when the Bucs won SB XXXVII. He was an analyst on ESPN's *Monday Night Football* before he returned to coaching with the Raiders in 2019.

3. John Madden is the Raiders all-time winningest head coach with a record of 103-32-7.

4. The Raiders organization does not retire jersey numbers. All 99 numbers are available, regardless of who once wore the number in the past.

5. Oakland, Las Vegas, and the Raiders have ever hosted the Super Bowl.

6. The Raiders' franchise is currently headquartered at the Intermountain Healthcare Performance Center in Henderson, Nevada.

7. The Raiders have made four Super Bowl appearances. They have faced the Minnesota Vikings, Philadelphia Eagles, Washington Redskins, and Tampa Bay Buccaneers.

8. The current owners of the Las Vegas Raiders are Mark and Carol Davis. When Al Davis died in 2011, control of the franchise went to his son Mark and Mark's wife, Carol.

9. The Raiders' mascot, Raider Rusher, originated from the Nickelodeon show *NFL Rush Zone: Guardians of the Core*.

10. The Raiders' cheerleading squad is known as the "Las Vegas Raiderettes."

CHAPTER 2:

JERSEYS & NUMBERS

QUIZ TIME!

1. The original Oakland Raiders uniforms were black and gold with gothic numerals, while the helmets were black with a white stripe and no logo.

    a. True
    b. False

2. What are the Raiders' current team colors?

    a. Black and white
    b. Silver and black
    c. Silver and white
    d. Black and gold

3. When Al Davis became head coach and general manager of the Raiders in 1963, he changed the team's colors to silver and black and added a logo to the helmet.

    a. True
    b. False

4. What uniform number did Howie Long wear as a member of the Raiders?

    a. 65
    b. 70
    c. 75
    d. 80

5. What uniform number does QB Derek Carr wear?

    a. 2
    b. 3
    c. 4
    d. 5

6. What uniform number did Sebastian Janikowski wear with the Raiders?

    a. 10
    b. 11
    c. 12
    d. 14

7. During his time with the Raiders, Ken Stabler wore No. 12.

    a. True
    b. False

8. What uniform number did Tim Brown wear during his time with the Raiders?

    a. 71
    b. 78
    c. 80
    d. 81

9. What uniform number did Marshawn Lynch wear when he was with the Raiders?

    a. 23
    b. 24
    c. 25
    d. 27

10. During his time with the Raiders, Marcus Allen wore No. 32.

    a. True
    b. False

11. What uniform number did Jim Otto for all but one year with the Raiders?

    a. 00
    b. 1
    c. 2
    d. 3

12. What uniform number did Gene Upshaw wear as a Raider?

    a. 60
    b. 61
    c. 63
    d. 65

13. During his time with the Raiders, Steve Wisniewski wore No. 67.

    a. True
    b. False

14. What uniform number did Willie Brown wear during his time with the Raiders?

    a. 22
    b. 24
    c. 25
    d. 25

15. What uniform number did Art Shell wear during his time with the Raiders?

    a. 68
    b. 70
    c. 78
    d. 87

16. What uniform number did Fred Biletnikoff wear with the Raiders?

    a. 14
    b. 25
    c. 32
    d. Both A & B

17. What uniform number did Cliff Branch wear as a Raider?

    a. 11
    b. 21
    c. 31
    d. 41

18. What uniform number did Terry McDaniel wear during his time with the Raiders?

    a. 16
    b. 26

c. 36

d. 46

19. What uniform number did Lester Hayes wear as a Raider?

    a. 7

    b. 17

    c. 27

    d. 37

20. The Raiders have retired five uniform numbers.

    a. True

    b. False

QUIZ ANSWERS

1. A - True

2. B – Silver and black

3. A – True

4. C – 75

5. C – 4

6. B – 11

7. A – True

8. D – 81

9. B – 24

10. A – True

11. A – 00

12. C – 63

13. B – False, 76

14. B – 24

15. C – 78

16. D – Both A & B

17. B – 21

18. C – 36

19. D – 37

20. B – False (0 because the Raiders do not retire uniform numbers.)

DID YOU KNOW?

1. The Raiders organization does not retire uniform numbers. All 99 numbers are available for any player to wear, regardless of who wore the number in the past.

2. During his time with the Raiders, Jerry Rice wore No. 80.

3. When he was with the Raiders, Charles Woodson wore No. 24.

4. Josh Jacobs currently wears No. 28 for the Las Vegas Raiders.

5. As a Raider, Bo Jackson wore No. 34.

6. The Raiders' current silver and black uniform design has essentially remained the same since it debuted in 1963. Their uniforms include silver helmets, silver pants, and either black or white jerseys.

7. The Raiders wore their white jerseys at home for the first time in their history on September 28, 2008, against the San Diego Chargers due to the heat in Oakland.

8. During the 2012 and 2013 seasons, the Raiders wore black cleats as a tribute to Al Davis. They went back to white cleats in 2014.

9. Despite moving from Oakland to Las Vegas in 2020, no changes to uniforms or logos were made except changing the word "Oakland" to "Las Vegas."

10. During 2016's Color Rush initiative, the Raiders wore white pants but retired them in 2018.

CHAPTER 3:

FAMOUS QUOTES

QUIZ TIME!

1. Which former Raiders player once said: "If something is said about the Raiders, I'm ready to go to war"?

   a. Randy Moss
   b. Charles Woodson
   c. Daryle Lamonica
   d. Jim Otto

2. Which former Raiders player once said: "Love yourself. Respect yourself. Never sell yourself short. Believe in yourself regardless of what people think. You can accomplish anything, absolutely anything, if you set your mind to it"?

   a. Gene Upshaw
   b. Marcus Allen
   c. Tim Brown
   d. Lester Hayes

3. Howie Long once said: "Winners, I am convinced, imagine their dreams first. They want it with all their heart and expect it to come true. There is, I believe, no other way to win."

    a. True
    b. False

4. Which Raiders head coach once said: "The fire that burns the brightest in the Raiders organization is the will to win"?

    a. Jon Gruden
    b. John Madden
    c. Al Davis
    d. Art Shell

5. Which former Raiders player once said: "Today I will do what others won't, so tomorrow I can accomplish what others can't"?

    a. Terry McDaniel
    b. Jerry Rice
    c. Willie Brown
    d. Marquette King

6. Which former Raiders player is quoted as saying: "Set your goals high and don't stop till you get there"?

    a. Fred Biletnikoff
    b. Rich Gannon
    c. Bo Jackson
    d. Jeff Jaeger

7. Which former Raiders quarterback is quoted as saying: "I am very proud of my association with the Oakland Raiders. I am very thankful to Mr. Davis for giving me that opportunity to play in 1999"?

    a. Rich Gannon
    b. Derek Carr
    c. Ken Stabler
    d. Daryle Lamonica

8. Former Raider Ken Stabler once said, "Pressure is something you feel when you don't know what the hell you're doing."

    a. True
    b. False

9. Which Raiders head coach once said: "The road to Easy Street goes through the sewer"?

    a. Jack Del Rio
    b. John Madden
    c. Dennis Allen
    d. Al Davis

10. "Just win, _____!" – Al Davis

    a. Team
    b. Raiders
    c. Baby
    d. Guys

11. Which former Raiders player is quoted as saying: "Al Davis treated me like a son. That man helped me become the man I am today"?

a. Charles Woodson

b. Darren McFadden

c. Jerry Rice

d. Sebastian Janikowski

12. Which celebrity is quoted as saying, "The silver and black may have another home, but the Raiders will always belong to the people of Los Angeles"?

a. Tom Hanks

b. George Lopez

c. Ice Cube

d. Larry King

13. Which celebrity is quoted as saying: "If you're from Oakland and you're not a Raiders fan, you're not from Oakland"?

a. Zendaya

b. Larry King

c. Jessica Alba

d. Ice Cube

14. Which MLB legend is quoted as saying: "My dream was to play football for the Oakland Raiders. But my mother thought I would get hurt playing football, so she chose baseball for me. I guess moms do know best"?

a. Derek Jeter

b. Rickey Henderson

c. Tony Gwynn

d. Frank Thomas

15. Which former Raiders player is quoted as saying, "Sports ideally teach discipline and commitment. They challenge you and build character for everything you do in life"?

    a. Jerry Rice
    b. Jack Tatum
    c. Howie Long
    d. Gene Upshaw

16. Former Raider Marcus Allen once said, "If you aren't going all the way, why go at all?"

    a. True
    b. False

17. Which former Raiders punter is quoted as saying: "I hope I inspire young punters to achieve their dreams to one day play in the NFL and maybe even be elected into the Hall of Fame"?

    a. Shane Lechler
    b. Marquette King
    c. A.J. Cole
    d. Ray Guy

18. Which former Raiders player is quoted as saying, "If you can believe it, the mind can achieve it"?

    a. Ronnie Lott
    b. Jerry Rice
    c. Bo Jackson
    d. Marcus Allen

19. Which former Raiders player once said: "I like to believe that my best hits border on felonious assault"?

    a. Howie Long

    b. Lester Hayes

    c. Jack Tatum

    d. Charles Woodson

20. When giving advice to younger players, former Raider Marshawn Lynch once said: "Take care of y'all mentals, y'all bodies, y'all chicken, so when y'all ready to walk away, y'all walk away and you'll be able to do what y'all want to do."

    a. True

    b. False

QUIZ ANSWERS

1. D – Jim Otto

2. B – Marcus Allen

3. B – False (Joe Montana)

4. C – Al Davis

5. B – Jerry Rice

6. C – Bo Jackson

7. A – Rich Gannon

8. B – False (Peyton Manning)

9. B – John Madden

10. C – Baby

11. D – Sebastian Janikowski

12. C – Ice Cube

13. A – Zendaya

14. B – Rickey Henderson

15. C – Howie Long

16. B – False, Joe Namath

17. D – Ray Guy

18. A – Ronnie Lott

19. C – Jack Tatum

20. A – True

DID YOU KNOW?

1. "Once a Raider, always a Raider." – Al Davis

2. "I always said that if I had one quarterback to make a drive the length of the field at the end of the game to win that game that guy would be Ken Stabler, number 12. We miss you, love you, and will see you in the Hall of Fame. It is my pleasure to present for enshrinement into the Pro Football Hall of Fame, my friend Ken Stabler." – John Madden's Speech at the late Ken Stabler's Pro Football Hall of Fame enshrinement

3. "Aside from my will to win, my commitment to excellence, the fire that burns brightest in me is the great love and enthusiasm that I have and had for the game of football and for everyone and everything connected with it. I love the game, I love the league, I love my team." – Al Davis in his Pro Football Hall of Fame enshrinement speech

4. "Wow, wow, wow. You know, you always think of what it would be like if you are ever enshrined into the Hall of Fame. People say, 'What are you going to say when you get up to the podium?' I tell them, 'I don't know. I'll tell you what I get up there.' And right now, I don't have I got like numb, you know, a tingle from the bottom of my toes to the top of my head. I mean, this is so special." – John Madden in his Pro Football Hall of Fame enshrinement speech

5. "I think back at the beginning of my career when a man named Al Davis drafted a kid out of Villanova in the second round, and at that time many of the football experts viewed that pick as a stretch, a reach, a surprise. But Al Davis saw something in me that many, including myself, did not. The Raiders were a team steeped in history. From the moment I walked into the Raider camp, I could feel it. It was all around me. People who not only defined what the Raiders were about, but also define what the National Football League was all about – John Madden, George Blanda, Ted Hendricks, Jim Otto, Willie Brown, Fred Biletnikoff, and Gene Upshaw and Art Shell helped bring me up. Then, of course, there was an owner named Al Davis, whose passion for winning was unparalleled in sports. So, it's understandable that when you're around people like that on a daily basis, you allow yourself to dream just a little bit. Albeit way in the back of your mind, dream of someday maybe being one of them. But at that time, taking the place of football history with those great men was just a dream and nothing more. I am extremely proud to have been a Raider. I am also proud to have played my entire career with the Raiders, something that rarely happens in today's game." – Howie Long in his Pro Football Hall of Fame enshrinement speech

6. "To the Los Angeles Raiders, I'd like to thank Mr. Al Davis for drafting me, Mr. Ron Wolf and Coach Tom Flores for putting his faith and trust in a rookie. Tom, I appreciate everything you did for me. And, to my position coach –

Ray Willsey. Some assistant coaches never get a lot of credit but thanks to Ray Willsey. He liberated me. He understood the power of words. My rookie season, and I am sure most football players assume that professional coaches know more than the college coaches so they're always willing to do exactly what they say, to please them, to endear ourselves to the coaching staff. Well, Ray Willsey never once told me 'don't.' He never once said 'don't run like this, don't run like that, don't catch like this, or don't catch like that.' Ray Willsey said to me, 'Make sure,' he says, 'Marcus, make sure you get the first down. Make sure you know the down and distance.' And that liberated me to be the expressive back that I was. And Ray, I see you back there in your shades. I never told you that but thank you very much." – Marcus Allen in his Pro Football Hall of Fame enshrinement speech

7. "I can never thank all the people who have helped me get here. I can't thank all the people who have had so much influence on my life. My teammates, there are too many, my friends, the media, the people in the Bay area, the people in Los Angeles, they have been very good to me. It has given me an opportunity to do some things that I never knew was possible, but I had the right upbringing, the right discipline. I had what it took because I was afraid to fail. Someone asked me 'what was it like to play for Al Davis, what was it like? Can you describe what it was like in 30 seconds?' Well, it takes longer than 30 seconds to describe Al Davis." – Gene Upshaw in his Pro Football Hall of Fame enshrinement speech

8. "In 1963, things began to change, and my dream was alive again and I thank God for bringing the right people into my dream again. At that time a young man was to become the head coach and general manager of the open Raiders and guide me where I am standing today, and that man is Al Davis. He sold me on the Raiders, not only that he sold me on myself. He along with Ollie Spencer as my line coach, John Madden as my head coach kept me motivated to playing some of the most exciting football games ever played in the National Football League. The great come-from-behind wins, the good plays for us, some of the fluke plays for the other teams…well, you remember some of those game, I don't have to tell you about those, they were a great part in making my dreams come true." – Jim Otto in his Pro Football Hall of Fame enshrinement speech

9. "I was fortunate to play in some of the greatest games in the history of the professional game. I played with some of the greatest players that ever played this game and I played against some of the greats as you see behind me and to my left. That is the ultimate. To play against these people, these great people who made this game what it is today, and I was glad to be one of those guys. I was coached by three of the greatest coaches of the Raiders history. John Rausch was one of my coaches. He led a team to the Super Bowl. John Madden was my second coach, he led a team to the Super Bowl and Tom Flores was my third coach and he also led a team to the Super Bowl, so that tells you what kind of coaches we had

coming through the organization as well as players. The Raider organization can be summed up in two words or two nouns, as you might say. Al Davis. He is the organization. The organization begins and it ends with him. His knowledge of the game is second to none. Every coach and every player that ever comes into this organization ever came through has gained some wealth from that knowledge. And to this day I am still gaining and trying to pick his brain as much as I can because there is a lot there to be had.

10. "This man has been an assistant coach in the NFL, he has been a head coach in the NFL, he has been a commissioner, now he is an owner and general partner. What else could anyone do in the game of football? He has done it all, he's done it all. There is not a time that any ex-player or coach can't pick up the phone and call him. You can call him at any time, even if you are not a Raider. If you are a fan, you can still call, and he will answer you. Some people call him a Darth Vader of professional football and he can be, he is a very tough man, he is a tough man to work for as a player and as a coach. But you know what, he has a soft side to him. Not too many people know about it unless you are a part of the Raider family.

11. "If you are a part of that Raider family, then you can understand what this man is all about. I love the man. The man has been good to me and my family. The man has been good to so many Raiders and their families and I love him for that. And, of course, we all know that behind

every man there is a good woman. His lovely wife is Carol Davis that epitomizes the courage and love the Raiders have for each other and that lady loves everybody. There is not a bad word that can be said about that lady, so she is special to me, she is like Mom and I appreciate it. I want to thank Al for making this occasion possible by having the courage to draft a guy from a small school, the patience to allow him to become a football player in the NFL, and also the courage to give him a job as an assistant football coach in the NFL." – Art Shell in his Pro Football Hall of Fame enshrinement speech

12. 10. "I would never have fulfilled the honor of being here today if it hadn't been for Al Davis, who at my age of 39 thought that I could still kick and throw the football a little bit. And when Al called me up in July of 1967 to come back and try out my third season, my third career with the Oakland Raiders, I was supposed to jump at it. Without Al and without the Raiders, without that team spirit out there with the pride and poise, the winning attitude and playing about 85% of the games in the nine years we won with the Raiders, certainly that attitude was very, very helpful to me. And without Al Davis and without this guidance at the top managing that club, I would not be here today. I want to thank two great coaches I had at Oakland, Johnny Rausch who was my coach in 1967 and 1968. He helped me; he also coached my brother at Army as quarterback coach. I also want to thank John Madden, who is here, who put on a great show yesterday and without John and

31

his leadership, I might not have been there for the seven years I played for John." – George Blanda in his Pro Football Hall of Fame enshrinement speech

CHAPTER 4:

CATCHY NICKNAMES

QUIZ TIME!

1. What nickname did Jack Tatum go by?

    a. The Sniper

    b. The Spy

    c. The Assassin

    d. The Killer

2. Daryle Lamonica was nicknamed "The Mad Bomber."

    a. True

    b. False

3. What was Ken Stabler's nickname?

    a. The Lizard

    b. The Snake

    c. The Tarantula

    d. The Wolf

4. What nickname does Marshawn Lynch go by?

    a. Oakland

    b. Skittles

c. Shawny L

d. Beast Mode

5. Which is NOT a nickname for the Raiders as a team?

   a. The Silver and Black

   b. The Men in Black

   c. America's Most Wanted

   d. The Legion of Raider Nation

6. What nickname did Tim Brown go by?

   a. Mr. T

   b. Mr. B

   c. Mr. Raider

   d. Mr. Oakland

7. Skip Thomas had the simple nickname "Dr. Death."

   a. True

   b. False

8. What nickname did Gene Upshaw go by?

   a. Highway 63

   b. Uptown Gene

   c. Downtown Gene

   d. Both A & B

9. What nickname did Fred Biletnikoff go by?

   a. Coyote

   b. Doctor Zhivago

   c. Werewolf

   d. Both A & B

10. "Bo" is a nickname. What is Bo Jackson's full name?

    a. Edward Vincent Jackson

    b. Vincent Edward Jackson

    c. Richard Vincent Jackson

    d. Edward Vincent Jackson

11. What nickname did Lester Hayes go by?

    a. Holy Hayes

    b. Crazy Legs Hayes

    c. The Lawyer

    d. The Judge

12. The Raiders cheerleaders are nicknamed "The Raiderettes."

    a. True

    b. False

13. What nickname did Charles Woodson go by?

    a. Woody

    b. Scratchy

    c. Poochie

    d. Itchy

14. What was Sebastian Janikowski's nickname?

    a. The Cuban Cannon

    b. The Polish Cannon

    c. The Russian Cannon

    d. The American Cannon

15. Allegiant Stadium was nicknamed "The Death Star" by Mark Davis.

    a. True
    b. False

16. What nickname does Jon Gruden go by?

    a. Jason
    b. Ghostface
    c. Freddie
    d. Chucky

17. The nickname given to Raiders fans is "Raider Nation."

    a. True
    b. False

18. What nickname did Steve Wisniewski go by?

    a. Win
    b. Ski
    c. The Wiz
    d. The Scarecrow

19. What nickname did Frank Hawkins go by?

    a. The Eagle
    b. The Hawk
    c. The Goose
    d. The Duck

20. Jerry Rice has many nicknames including "GOAT," "World," "Flash 80," and "Gentleman Jerry."

    a. True
    b. False

QUIZ ANSWERS

1. C – The Assassin

2. A – True

3. B – The Snake

4. D – Beast Mode

5. D – The Legion of Raider Nation

6. C – Mr. Raider

7. A – True

8. D – Both A & B

9. D – Both A & B

10. B – Vincent Edward Jackson

11. D – The Judge

12. A – True

13. C – Poochie

14. B – The Polish Cannon

15. A – True

16. D – Chucky

17. A – True

18. C – The Wiz

19. B – The Hawk

20. A – True

DID YOU KNOW?

1. Former Raider Jeff Hostetler went by the nickname "Hoss."

2. Former Raider Latavius Murray has the nickname "Tay Train."

3. Former Raider Darren McFadden goes by the nickname "Run DMC."

4. "Ray-Ray" is a nickname. Former Raider Ray-Ray Armstrong's full name is Aravious Armstrong.

5. Current Raider Jalen Richard is nicknamed "Rocket."

6. Former Raider Doug Martin goes by the nickname "Muscle Hamster."

7. NFL Network gave current Raider Hunter Renfrow his nickname, "The Slot Machine."

8. Former Raider T.J. Houshmandzadeh's full name is Touraj Houshmandzadeh Jr.

9. Former Raider Rock Cartwright's full name is Roderick Rashaun Cartwright.

10. Former Raider Rich Gannon goes by the nickname "Loose Gannon."

CHAPTER 5:

CARR

QUIZ TIME!

1. What is Derek Carr's full name?

    a. Derek David Carr

    b. David Derek Carr

    c. Dallas Derek Carr

    d. Derek Dallas Carr

2. As of the 2020 season, Derek Carr has played his entire NFL career with the Raiders.

    a. True

    b. False

3. Where was Derek Carr born?

    a. Reno, Nevada

    b. Fresno, California

    c. Dallas, Texas

    d. Seattle, Washington

4. When was Derek Carr born?

    a. December 28, 1991
    b. December 28, 1993
    c. March 28, 1991
    d. March 28, 1993

5. Derek Carr is the younger brother of former 1st overall, NFL draft pick and current NFL analyst David Carr.

    a. True
    b. False

6. How many Pro Bowls has Derek Carr been named to in his career so far (as of the end of the 2019 season)?

    a. 1
    b. 3
    c. 5
    d. 6

7. Where did Derek Carr go to college?

    a. Stanford University
    b. CSU Bakersfield
    c. Fresno State University
    d. San Diego State University

8. Derek Carr was drafted by the Oakland Raiders in the 2nd round of the 2014 NFL draft.

    a. True
    b. False

9. Who was Derek Carr's brother, David, drafted by?

    a. Oakland Raiders

    b. New York Giants

    c. San Francisco 49ers

    d. Houston Texans

10. How many Super Bowls has Derek Carr started (as of the end of the 2019 season)?

    a. 0

    b. 1

    c. 2

    d. 3

11. Derek Carr holds the Raiders record for most passing yards in a game, with how many, on October 30, 2016, against the Tampa Bay Buccaneers?

    a. 501

    b. 510

    c. 513

    d. 515

12. Derek Carr started at quarterback in all 16 games for the Raiders in 2014, his rookie season.

    a. True

    b. False

13. How many times has Derek Carr been named the AFC Offensive Player of the Week (as of the end of the 2019 season)?

    a. 0

    b. c. 1

c. d. 2

d. e. 3

14. Derek Carr and Heather, his wife since 2012, have three sons.

    a. True

    b. False

15. Derek Carr holds the Raiders record for most touchdown passes in a game with, how many, on October 12, 2014, against the San Diego Chargers?

    a. 3

    b. 4

    c. 5

    d. 6

16. How many times was Derek Carr named the Mountain West Conference Offensive Player of the Year?

    a. 0

    b. 1

    c. 2

    d. 3

17. Derek Carr's uncle, Lon Boyett, played tight end for the Raiders during the 1978 season.

    a. True

    b. False

18. How many Super Bowl championships has Carr won during his career so far (as of the end of the 2019 season)?

a. 0

b. 1

c. 2

d. 3

19. What number does Derek Carr currently wear?

a. 1

b. 4

c. 14

d. 40

20. While at Fresno State, Derek Carr wore No. 4 to honor his favorite NFL player, Brett Favre.

a. True

b. False

QUIZ ANSWERS

1. D – Derek Dallas Carr

2. A – True

3. B – Fresno, California

4. C – March 28, 1991

5. A - True

6. B – 3

7. C – Fresno State University

8. A – True

9. D – Houston Texans

10. A – 0

11. C – 513

12. A – True

13. B – 1 (Week 8, 2016)

14. A – True

15. B – 4

16. C – 2 (2012, 2013)

17. A - True

18. B – 1

19. B – 4

20. A – True

DID YOU KNOW?

1. Derek Carr's No. 4 was retired by the Fresno State Bulldogs during halftime of a game in 2017.

2. On July 14, 2019, Derek Carr received a mural at Fresno State University.

3. In 2014, his rookie season, Carr became the first Raiders quarterback to start all 16 games since Rich Gannon in 2002.

4. In his first-ever NFL game, Derek Carr faced the New York Jets. He passed for 151 yards and 2 touchdowns.

5. Derek Carr was named to the list of Top 100 NFL players in 2016, 2017, and 2018.

6. Derek Carr won the 2013 Sammy Baugh Trophy, which is given annually to the nation's top collegiate passer.

7. In college, Derek Carr was named a 2x (2012 and 2013) First-Team All-MWC (Mountain West Conference).

8. Derek Carr was named the Week 5 FedEx Air Player of the Week in 2020.

9. Derek Carr threw the most touchdowns of his career (so far) in 2015 with 32.

10. Derek Carr's oldest son was born with a medical condition that tied up his intestines and required three surgeries to fix.

CHAPTER 6:

STATISTICALLY SPEAKING

QUIZ TIME!

1. Tim Brown holds the Raiders franchise record for the most career receiving touchdowns with _how many?

   a. 71
   b. 85
   c. 99
   d. 120

2. Art Powell holds the franchise record for the most receiving touchdowns in a season with 16 in 1963.

   a. True
   b. False

3. Marcus Allen holds the franchise record for the most career rushing touchdowns with how many?

   a. 69
   b. 79
   c. 89
   d. 99

4. Charles Woodson holds the franchise record for the most forced fumbles with how many?

    a. 8
    b. 10
    c. 15
    d. 18

5. Which player holds the Raiders record for most sacks in a season with 16 in 2005?

    a. Warren Sapp
    b. Charles Woodson
    c. Derrick Burgess
    d. Tommy Kelly

6. Who is the team's all-time career passing leader with 22,793 yards?

    a. Ken Stabler
    b. Daryle Lamonica
    c. Rich Gannon
    d. Derek Carr

7. Current Las Vegas Raiders quarterback Derek Carr holds the franchise record for most career pass completions with 2,120.

    a. True
    b. False

8. Pete Banaszak holds the franchise record for most rushing touchdowns in a single season (1975) with how many?

    a. 10
    b. 12

c. 16

d. 18

9. Tim Brown holds the franchise record for most receiving yards in a season with 1,408 in what year?

   a. 1995

   b. 1996

   c. 1997

   d. 1999

10. Rich Gannon holds the team's record for most passing yards in a single season with 4,689 in what year?

    a. 1999

    b. 2002

    c. 2003

    d. 2004

11. Who holds the Raiders franchise record for passing touchdowns in a single season with 34 in 1969.

    a. George Blanda

    b. Ken Stabler

    c. Jim Plunkett

    d. Daryle Lamonica

12. Lester Hayes holds the team record for pass interceptions in a single season with 13 in 1980.

    a. True

    b. False

13. Jeff Jaeger holds the franchise record for field goals made in a single season in 1993, with how many?

a. 25

b. 35

c. 45

d. 55

14. Tim Brown holds the Raiders record for receptions in a single season in 1997, with how many?

    a. 84

    b. 94

    c. 104

    d. 114

15. Willie Brown and Lester Hayes are tied for the franchise record for career pass interceptions with how many each?

    a. 29

    b. 30

    c. 35

    d. 39

16. Marcus Allen holds the team's record for touchdowns in a single season, in 1984, with how many?

    a. 15

    b. 18

    c. 20

    d. 22

17. Tim Brown holds the franchise record for career touchdowns with 104.

    a. True

    b. False

18. Sebastian Janikowski holds the Raiders record for career field goals made with how many?

    a. 214
    b. 314
    c. 414
    d. 514

19. Sebastian Janikowski holds the team's record for career points with how many?

    a. 1,699
    b. 1,799
    c. 1,899
    d. 1,999

20. Sebastian Janikowski holds the Las franchise record for points in a single season with 142 in 2010.

    a. True
    b. False

QUIZ ANSWERS

1. C – 99

2. A – True

3. B – 79

4. D – 18

5. C – Derrick Burgess

6. D – Derek Carr

7. A – True

8. C – 16

9. C – 1997

10. B – 2002

11. D – Daryle Lamonica

12. A – True

13. B – 35

14. C – 104

15. D – 39

16. B – 18

17. A – True

18. C – 414

19. B – 1,799

20. A – True

DID YOU KNOW?

1. Ken Stabler holds the Raiders franchise record for career passing touchdowns with 150.

2. Shane Lechler holds the franchise record for career punt yardage with 148,215. yards.

3. Marquette King holds the Raiders record for punt yardage in a single season with 4,930. yards in 2014.

4. John Madden holds the franchise record for wins as a head coach with 103.

5. Marcus Allen holds the Raiders record with 8,545 career rushing yards. Allen also holds the Raiders single season record for rushing yards with 1,759 in 1985.

6. Greg Townsend holds the franchise record for career sacks with 107.5.

7. Chris Carr holds the Raiders franchise record for career kickoff return yards with 4,841 yards. Carr also holds the Raiders record for kickoff return yards in a single season with 1,762 in 2006.

8. Tim Brown holds the Raiders record for career punt return yards with 3,272 yards.

9. Fulton Walker holds the team record for punt return yards in a single season with 692 yards in 1985.

10. Charles Woodson holds the franchise record for career pass deflections with 84.

CHAPTER 7:

THE TRADE MARKET

QUIZ TIME!

1. On March 13, 2019, the Oakland Raiders traded 2019 3rd-round pick Diontae Johnson and 2019 5th-round pick Zach Gentry to the Pittsburgh Steelers in exchange for who?

    a. Hunter Renfrow

    b. Antonio Brown

    c. Rico Gafford

    d. Jalen Richard

2. On April 27, 2019, the Oakland Raiders traded 2019 5th-round pick Michael Jackson and a 2019 7th-round draft pick Mike Weber to which team, in exchange for a 2019 5th-round draft pick (Hunter Renfrow) in a draft pick switch?

    a. Cleveland Browns

    b. Detroit Lions

    c. Indianapolis Colts

    d. Dallas Cowboys

3. On September 1, 2018, the Oakland Raiders traded Khalil Mack to the Chicago Bears in exchange for the draft pick that allowed them to draft Josh Jacobs.

   a. True
   b. False

4. On October 22, 2018, the Oakland Raiders traded Amari Cooper to the which team in exchange for 2019 1st-round draft pick Johnathan Abram?

   a. New York Jets
   b. Dallas Cowboys
   c. San Francisco 49ers
   d. Miami Dolphins

5. On April 21, 2014, the Oakland Raiders traded Terrelle Pryor to the Seattle Seahawks in exchange for a 2014 7th-round draft pick (Jonathan Dowling).

   a. True
   b. False

6. On March 30, 2012, the Oakland Raiders traded Bruce Campbell to the which team in exchange for Mike Goodson?

   a. New York Giants
   b. New York Jets
   c. Carolina Panthers
   d. San Diego Chargers

7. On October 18, 2011, the Oakland Raiders traded a 2012 1st-round draft pick and a 2013 2nd-round draft pick to the Cincinnati Bengals in exchange for whom?

a. Jacoby Ford
b. Darren McFadden
c. Aaron Curry
d. Carson Palmer

8. On April 23, 2010, the Oakland Raiders traded which 2010 2nd-round draft pick to the New England Patriots in exchange for 2010 2nd-round draft pick Lamarr Houston and 2010 6th-round draft pick Travis Goethel?

a. Aaron Hernandez
b. Rob Gronkowski
c. Tom Brady
d. Julian Edelman

9. On April 24, 2010, the Oakland Raiders traded Kirk Morrison and 2010 5th-round draft pick Austen Lane to which team, in exchange for 2010 4th-round draft pick Jacoby Ford?

a. Buffalo Bills
b. Detroit Lions
c. Jacksonville Jaguars
d. Chicago Bears

10. On September 6, 2009, the Oakland Raiders traded a 2011 1st-round draft pick (Nate Solder) to the New England Patriots in exchange for Richard Seymour.

a. True
b. False

11. On October 19, 2004, the Oakland Raiders traded which player to the Seattle Seahawks in exchange for an undisclosed 2004 draft pick?

   a. Rich Gannon
   b. Ronald Curry
   c. Charles Woodson
   d. Jerry Rice

12. On August 28, 1994, the Los Angeles Raiders traded Charles Jordan to the Green Bay Packers in exchange for a 1995 5th-round draft pick (Rich Owens).

   a. True
   b. False

13. On May 13, 1996, the Oakland Raiders traded 1997 5th-round draft pick Keith Thibodeaux to which team in exchange for Lincoln Kennedy?

   a. Minnesota Vikings
   b. Washington Redskins
   c. Atlanta Falcons
   d. Green Bay Packers

14. On August 24, 1999, the Oakland Raiders traded a 2000 6th-round draft pick (John Frank) to the Philadelphia Eagles in exchange for Bobby Hoying.

   a. True
   b. False

15. On August 27, 2000, the Oakland Raiders traded Chuck Osborne to the which team in exchange for an undisclosed 2002 draft pick?

a. St. Louis Rams

b. San Diego Chargers

c. Pittsburgh Steelers

d. Green Bay Packers

16. On April 21, 2001, the Oakland Raiders traded 2001 4th-round draft pick Marcus Bell to which team, in exchange for Roland Williams?

a. Arizona Cardinals

b. St. Louis Rams

c. Detroit Lions

d. Kansas City Chiefs

17. What team did the Oakland Raiders acquire Matt Flynn from on April 1, 2013, in a draft pick switch?

a. Green Bay Packers

b. Seattle Seahawks

c. Buffalo Bills

d. Denver Broncos

18. On September 11, 2004, the Oakland Raiders traded Chris Cooper to the which team in exchange for an undisclosed 2004 draft pick?

a. Dallas Cowboys

b. Atlanta Falcons

c. San Francisco 49ers

d. Arizona Cardinals

19. On March 3, 2005, the Oakland Raiders traded Napoleon Harris, 2005 1st-round draft pick Troy Williamson, and

2005 7th-round draft pick Adrian Ward to the Minnesota Vikings in exchange for which player?

   a. Charles Woodson

   b. Shane Lechler

   c. Randy Moss

   d. Warren Sapp

20. On April 16, 2018, the Oakland Raiders traded Sebastian Janikowski to the Seattle Seahawks.

   a. True

   b. False

QUIZ ANSWERS

1. B – Antonio Brown

2. D – Dallas Cowboys

3. A – True

4. B – Dallas Cowboys

5. A – True

6. C – Carolina Panthers

7. D – Carson Palmer

8. B – Rob Gronkowski

9. C – Jacksonville Jaguars

10. A – True

11. D – Jerry Rice

12. A – True

13. C – Atlanta Falcons

14. A – True

15. D – Green Bay Packers

16. B – St. Louis Rams

17. B – Seattle Seahawks

18. A – Dallas Cowboys

19. C – Randy Moss

20. B – False (Janikowski signed with the Seahawks as a free agent.)

DID YOU KNOW?

1. On September 2, 2006, the Oakland Raiders traded Bobby Hamilton to the New York Jets in exchange for a 2008 7th-round draft pick.

2. On April 29, 2007, the Oakland Raiders traded Randy Moss to the New England Patriots in exchange for a 2007 4th-round draft pick (John Bowie).

3. On August 20, 2007, the Oakland Raiders traded an undisclosed 2007 draft pick to the Denver Broncos in exchange for Gerard Warren.

4. On August 7, 2009, the Oakland Raiders traded Derrick Burgess to the New England Patriots in exchange for an undisclosed 2009 draft pick.

5. On October 14, 2011, the Oakland Raiders traded a 2012 7th-round draft pick (J.R. Sweezy) and a 2013 5th-round draft pick (Tharold Simon) to the Seattle Seahawks in exchange for Aaron Curry.

6. On April 27, 2013, the Oakland Raiders traded a 2013 4th-round draft pick (Akeem Spence) to the Tampa Bay Buccaneers in exchange for a 2013 4th-round draft pick (Tyler Wilson) and a 2013 6th-round draft pick (Latavius Murray).

7. On March 21, 2014, the Oakland Raiders traded a 2014 6th-round draft pick (Alfred Blue) to the Houston Texans in exchange for Matt Schaub.

8. On September 3, 2016, the Oakland Raiders traded Dewey McDonald to the Seattle Seahawks in exchange for a 2017 7th-round draft pick (Treyvon Hester).

9. On April 28, 2018, the Oakland Raiders traded Jihad Ward to the Dallas Cowboys In exchange for Ryan Switzer.

10. On October 8, 2019, the Oakland Raiders traded a 2012 5th-round draft pick to the Buffalo Bills in exchange for Zay Jones.

CHAPTER 8:

DRAFT DAY

QUIZ TIME!

1. With the 36th overall pick, of which round of the 2014 NFL draft, did the Oakland Raiders select QB Derek Carr?

   a. 2nd
   b. 3rd
   c. 4th
   d. 5th

2. With the 17th overall pick, in the 1st round the NFL draft of what year, did the Oakland Raiders selected Sebastian Janikowski?

   a. 1998
   b. 1999
   c. 2000
   d. 2002

3. With the 12th overall pick, in the 1st round of the 2007 NFL draft, which team selected Marshawn Lynch?

   a. Seattle Seahawks
   b. Oakland Raiders

c. San Francisco 49ers

d. Buffalo Bills

4. With the 16th overall pick, in 1st round of the 1985 NFL draft, which team selected Jerry Rice?

    a. Oakland Raiders

    b. Denver Broncos

    c. San Francisco 49ers

    d. Seattle Seahawks

5. With the 48th overall pick, in the 2nd round of the NFL draft, in what year did the Oakland Raiders select Howie Long?

    a. 1980

    b. 1981

    c. 1983

    d. 1984

6. With which pick overall, in the 2nd round of the 1968 NFL draft, did the Oakland Raiders select Ken Stabler?

    a. 39th

    b. 46th

    c. 52nd

    d. 55th

7. With the 10th overall pick, in the 1st round of the 1982 NFL draft, the Los Angeles Raiders selected Marcus Allen.

    a. True

    b. False

8. With which pick overall, in the 1st round of the 1998 NFL draft, did the Oakland Raiders select Charles Woodson?

    a. 1st
    b. 2nd
    c. 3rd
    d. 4th

9. With the 17th overall pick, in the 1st round of the NFL draft in what year did the Oakland Raiders selected Gene Upshaw?

    a. 1965
    b. 1967
    c. 1968
    d. 1969

10. The Los Angeles Raiders drafted Tim Brown in the 1st round, 6th overall, in the 1988 NFL draft.

    a. True
    b. False

11. With the 29th overall pick, in the 2nd round of the 1989 NFL draft, which team selected Steve Wisniewski?

    a. Oakland Raiders
    b. Pittsburgh Steelers
    c. Miami Dolphins
    d. Dallas Cowboys

12. Mychal Rivera was drafted in the 6th round, 184th overall, of the 2013 NFL draft by the Oakland Raiders.

    a. True
    b. False

13. With the 80th overall pick, in the 3rd round of the 1968 NFL draft, the Oakland Raiders selected which player?

    a. Willie Brown

    b. Jim Otto

    c. Art Shell

    d. Bo Jackson

14. In what round of the 1972 NFL draft, did the Oakland Raiders select Cliff Branch?

    a. 8th

    b. 4th

    c. 2nd

    d. 1st

15. With which overall pick, in the 1st round of the 1998 NFL draft, did the Los Angeles Raiders select Terry McDaniel?

    a. 3rd

    b. 5th

    c. 7th

    d. 9th

16. With the 136th overall pick, in the 4th round of the 2016 NFL draft, which team selected Devontae Booker?

    a. Denver Broncos

    b. Oakland Raiders

    c. Green Bay Packers

    d. Seattle Seahawks

17. With the 149th overall pick, in the 5th round of the 2019 NFL draft, the Oakland Raiders selected which player?

a. Alec Ingold

b. Hunter Renfrow

c. Zay Jones

d. Henry Ruggs III

18. Michael Crabtree was drafted in the 1st round, 10th overall, of the 2009 NFL draft by which team?

    a. Baltimore Ravens

    b. Arizona Cardinals

    c. San Francisco 49ers

    d. Oakland Raiders

19. With which overall pick, in the 1st round of the 2007 NFL draft, did the Oakland Raiders select Jamarcus Russell?

    a. 1st

    b. 2nd

    c. 3rd

    d. 4th

20. Rich Gannon was selected by the Oakland Raiders in the 4th round, 98th overall, in the 1987 NFL draft.

    a. True

    b. False

QUIZ ANSWERS

1. A – 2nd

2. C – 2000

3. D – Buffalo Bills

4. C – San Francisco 49ers

5. B – 1981

6. C – 52nd

7. A – True

8. D – 4th

9. B – 1967

10. A – True

11. D – Dallas Cowboys

12. A – True

13. C – Art Shell

14. B – 4th

15. D – 9th

16. A – Denver Broncos

17. B – Hunter Renfrow

18. C – San Francisco 49ers

19. A – 1st

20. B – False (New England Patriots)

DID YOU KNOW?

1. Former Raider Darren McFadden was selected by the Oakland Raiders in the 1st round, 4th overall, in the 2008 NFL draft.

2. Former Raider Fred Biletnikoff was selected by the Detroit Lions in the 3rd round, 39th overall, in the 1965 NFL draft.

3. Former Raider Daryle Lamonica was selected by the Green Bay Packers in the 12th round, 168th overall, in the 1963 NFL draft.

4. Former Raider Lester Hayes was selected by the Oakland Raiders in the 5th round, 126th overall, in the 1977 NFL draft.

5. Former Raider Jim Plunkett was selected by the New England Patriots in the 1st round, 1st overall, in the 1971 NFL draft.

6. Former Raider Ray Guy was selected by the Oakland Raiders in the 1st round, 23rd overall, in the 1973 NFL draft.

7. Former Raider Amari Cooper was selected by the Oakland Raiders in the 1st round, 4th overall, in the 2015 NFL draft.

8. Former Raider Bo Jackson was selected by the Los Angeles Raiders in the 7th round, 183rd overall, in the 1987 NFL draft.

9. Former Raider Todd Christensen was selected by the Dallas Cowboys in the 2nd round, 56th overall, in the 1978 NFL draft.

10. Former Raider Warren Sapp was selected by the Tampa Bay Buccaneers in the 1st round, 12th overall, in the 1995 NFL draft.

CHAPTER 9:

ODDS & ENDS

QUIZ TIME!

1. Which former Raiders player did NOT appear on Dancing with the Stars?

   a. Jerry Rice
   b. Rashad Jennings
   c. Howie Long
   d. Warren Sapp

2. Jerry Rice finished in the top two of the 2005-2006 season of Dancing with the Stars.

   a. True
   b. False

3. Gene Upshaw is the only player in NFL history to reach the Super Bowl in how many different decades with the same team?

   a. 2
   b. 3
   c. 4
   d. 5

4. In May 2019, Marshawn Lynch was cast in the third season of which television show, that premiered in 2020?

    a. Schitt's Creek
    b. The Mandalorian
    c. Stranger Things
    d. Westworld

5. After retiring from football, what became Napoleon Kaufman's second career?

    a. Real estate investor
    b. Motivational speaker
    c. Ordained minister
    d. Mattress salesman

6. Tim Brown was the first wide receiver to win the which award?

    a. Walter Payton Man of the Year Award
    b. NFL Rookie of the Year Award
    c. Walter Camp Award
    d. Heisman Trophy

7. Willie Brown is the grandfather of current NFL player Antonio Brown.

    a. True
    b. False

8. Which former Raiders player became their wide receiver coach from 1989-2007?

    a. Fred Biletnikoff
    b. Jerry Rice

    c. Cliff Branch

    d. Tim Brown

9. Which rapper has a song entitled "Raider Nation"?

    a. Jay-Z

    b. Ice Cube

    c. Drake

    d. Eminem

10. What is the name of Charles Woodson's Napa Valley wine label?

    a. Woodson Wine

    b. Just Wine Baby

    c. Twentyfour by Charles Woodson

    d. CW Wines

11. Sebastian Janikowski is one of only how many placekickers to be selected in the first round of the NFL draft?

    a. 2

    b. 3

    c. 4

    d. 5

12. Howie Long is a studio analyst for FOX Sports' NFL coverage.

    a. True

    b. False

13. Which 1990's sitcom did Bo Jackson NOT make an appearance on?

a. The Fresh Prince of Bel-Air

b. Moesha

c. Married… With Children

d. Full House

14. Ronnie Lott owns a car dealership for which brand?

a. Mercedes-Benz

b. Toyota

c. Ford

d. Both A & B

15. Former Raider turned actor Nnamdi Asomugha is married to which actress?

a. Halle Berry

b. Kerry Washington

c. Tamera Mowry

d. Gabrielle Union

16. George Blanda was the first-ever recorded fantasy football draft pick.

a. True

b. False

17. Former Raiders head coach John Madden has won how many Emmy Awards for his sportscasting work?

a. 6

b. 10

c. 16

d. 20

18. Ted Hendricks was the first Guatemalan-born NFL player.

    a. True
    b. False

19. What is the name of Marshawn Lynch's cellphone service, which he launched in 2017, which allows subscribers to pay their phone bill by engaging in ads and offers?

    a. Beast Mode Mobile
    b. Beast Mobile
    c. Money Mobile
    d. Marshawn Mobile

20. Former Raider Mychal Rivera is the brother of late Glee actress, Naya Rivera.

    a. True
    b. False

QUIZ ANSWERS

1. C – Howie Long

2. A – True

3. B – 3

4. D - Westworld

5. C – Ordained minister

6. D – Heisman Trophy

7. B – False

8. A – Fred Biletnikoff

9. B – Ice Cube

10. C – Twentyfour by Charles Woodson

11. B – 3

12. A – True

13. D – Full House

14. D – Both A & B

15. B – Kerry Washington

16. A – True

17. C – 16

18. A – True

19. B – Beast Mobile

20. A – True

DID YOU KNOW?

1. Al Davis was active in civil rights, refusing to allow the Raiders to play in any city where black and white players had to stay in separate hotels. He remains the only executive in NFL history to be an assistant coach, head coach, general manager, commissioner, and owner.

2. Gene Upshaw died of pancreatic cancer. There is now a cancer center in Truckee, California, called the "Gene Upshaw Memorial Tahoe Forest Cancer Center."

3. Marshawn Lynch attended the same Oakland high school as Oakland Athletics MLB legend Rickey Henderson: Oakland Technical High School.

4. In 2004, Steve Wisniewski was inducted into the National Polish-American Sports Hall of Fame.

5. Rod Martin was featured on the cover of *Sports Illustrated Magazine* after his record three interceptions in Super Bowl XV.

6. In March 2018, Phil Villapiano joined former NFL players Harry Carson and Nick Buoniconti to support an initiative called "Flag Football Under 14," which recommends no tackle football below that age out of a concern for the brain health of the young players.

7. After the death of President John F. Kennedy, Lincoln Kennedy remarked on ESPN's SportsCenter, "My name's

Lincoln Kennedy, I ain't got a chance," referring to the assassinations of Presidents Abraham Lincoln and Kennedy.

8. During the MLB Lockout in 1990, former Raider Todd Christensen tried out for the Oakland Athletics.

9. Bo Jackson played in the NFL for the Raiders and in MLB for the Kansas City Royals, Chicago White Sox, and California Angels.

10. Jim Otto pushed his body during his NFL career which resulted in nearly 74 operations, including 28 knee surgeries.

CHAPTER 10:

OFFENSE

QUIZ TIME!

1. How many Pro Bowls was Ken Stabler named to during his 15-season NFL career?

    a. 2

    b. 4

    c. 6

    d. 8

2. Marcus Allen played his entire 16-season NFL career with the Raiders.

    a. True

    b. False

3. Which of the following teams did former Raider Randy Moss NOT play for during his 16-season NFL career?

    a. Minnesota Vikings

    b. New England Patriots

    c. Green Bay Packers

    d. San Francisco 49ers

4. Former Raider Bo Jackson also played Major League Baseball.

    a. True
    b. False

5. What year was Jerry Rice inducted into the Pro Football Hall of Fame?

    a. 2004
    b. 2007
    c. 2008
    d. 2010

6. How many touchdowns did Fred Biletnikoff score during his 1969 season with the Oakland Raiders?

    a. 10
    b. 11
    c. 12
    d. 14

7. Steve Wisniewski played his entire 13-season NFL career with the Raiders.

    a. True
    b. False

8. During his seven-season NFL career, Rashad Jennings played for the Raiders, Jacksonville Jaguars, and which other team?

    a. Arizona Cardinals
    b. Detroit Lions
    c. Chicago Bears
    d. New York Giants

9. How many seasons did Michael Crabtree play for the Oakland Raiders?

    a. 1
    b. 2
    c. 3
    d. 4

10. Which of the following teams did Former Raider Rich Gannon NOT play for during his 17-season NFL career?

    a. Minnesota Vikings
    b. Kansas City Chiefs
    c. Dallas Cowboys
    d. Washington Redskins

11. How many Super Bowls did Jeff Hostetler win?

    a. 0
    b. 1
    c. 2
    d. 3

12. During his 13-season NFL career, Marshawn Lynch played for the Oakland Raiders, Seattle Seahawks, and Buffalo Bills.

    a. True
    b. False

13. How many Pro Bowls has current Las Vegas Raiders quarterback Derek Carr been named to (as of the end of the 2019 season)?

    a. 0
    b. 1

c. 2

d. 3

14. How many seasons did Jerry Rice play for the Oakland Raiders?

    a. 1

    b. 2

    c. 4

    d. 16

15. How many Super Bowl championships did Kenny King win in his seven-season NFL career?

    a. 1

    b. 2

    c. 3

    d. 4

16. How many Pro Bowls was Carson Palmer named to in his 14-season NFL career?

    a. 2

    b. 3

    c. 6

    d. 9

17. During his 12-season NFL career, Daryle Lamonica played for the Oakland Raiders and which other team?

    a. Tennessee Titans

    b. New York Jets

    c. Carolina Panthers

    d. Buffalo Bills

18. How many seasons did Terrelle Pryor play for the Oakland Raiders?

    a. 2
    b. 3
    c. 5
    d. 7

19. How many touchdowns did Jared Cook record during his 2018 season with the Oakland Raiders?

    a. 3
    b. 4
    c. 6
    d. 9

20. Randy Moss was inducted into the Pro Football Hall of Fame in 2018.

    a. True
    b. False

QUIZ ANSWERS

1. B – 4

2. B – False (Raiders and Kansas City Chiefs)

3. C – Green Bay Packers

4. A – True

5. D – 2010

6. C – 12

7. A – True

8. D – New York Giants

9. C – 3

10. C – Dallas Cowboys

11. C – 2

12. A – True

13. D – 3

14. C – 4

15. B – 2

16. B – 3

17. D – Buffalo Bills

18. B – 3

19. C – 6

20. A – True

DID YOU KNOW?

1. Current Raiders quarterback Derek Carr has been with the team since 2014. He has been named to three Pro Bowls.

2. Ken Stabler spent 10 years of his NFL career with the Oakland Raiders. He also played for the Houston Oilers and New Orleans Saints. He is a member of the Pro Football Hall of Fame, a 4x Pro Bowler, 1x All-Pro, 1x Super Bowl champion, and 1x MVP.

3. Randy Moss spent two years of his NFL career with the Oakland Raiders. He also played for the Minnesota Vikings, New England Patriots, San Francisco 49ers, and Tennessee Titans. He is a member of the Pro Football Hall of Fame, a 6x Pro Bowler, and 4x All-Pro.

4. Jerry Rice spent four years of his NFL career with the Oakland Raiders. He also played for the San Francisco 49ers and Seattle Seahawks. He is a member of the Pro Football Hall of Fame, a 13x Pro Bowler, 10x All-Pro, 3x Super Bowl champion, member of the HOF All-1980's team, member of the HOF All-1990's team, 1987 AP Offensive Player of the Year Award winner, 1993 AP Offensive Player of the Year Award winner, and 1987 Bert Bell Award winner.

5. Fred Biletnikoff spent his entire NFL career with the Oakland Raiders. He is a member of the Pro Football Hall of Fame, a 6x Pro Bowler, 2x All-Pro, and 1x Super Bowl champion.

6. Daryle Lamonica spent eight years of his NFL career with the Oakland Raiders. He also played for the Buffalo Bills. He is a 5x Pro Bowler and 2x All-Pro.

7. Rich Gannon spent six years of his NFL career with the Oakland Raiders. He also played for the Minnesota Vikings, Kansas City Chiefs, and Washington Redskins. He is a 4x Pro Bowler, 2x All-Pro, and 1x MVP.

8. Steve Wisniewski spent his entire NFL career with the LA/Oakland Raiders. He is an 8x Pro Bowler and 2x All-Pro.

9. Marcus Allen spent 11 years of his NFL career with the Oakland Raiders. He also played for the Kansas City Chiefs. He is a member of the Pro Football Hall of Fame, a 6x Pro Bowler, 2x All-Pro, 1x Super Bowl champion, and 1x MVP.

10. Marshawn Lynch spent two years of his NFL career with the Oakland Raiders. He also played for the Seattle Seahawks and Buffalo Bills. He is a 5x Pro Bowler, 1x All-Pro, and 1x Super Bowl champion.

CHAPTER 11:

DEFENSE

QUIZ TIME!

1. What year was Jim Otto inducted into the Pro Football Hall of Fame?

    a. 1975
    b. 1976
    c. 1980
    d. 1985

2. Jim Otto played his entire 15-season NFL career with the Oakland Raiders.

    a. True
    b. False

3. How many Pro Bowls was Charles Woodson named to during his 18-season NFL career?

    a. 6
    b. 9
    c. 11
    d. 15

4. What year was Howie Long inducted into the Pro Football Hall of Fame?

    a. 1995
    b. 1999
    c. 2000
    d. 2003

5. How many Super Bowl championships did Ronnie Lott win during his 14-season NFL career?

    a. 0
    b. 1
    c. 3
    d. 4

6. How many seasons did Matt Millen play for the LA/Oakland Raiders?

    a. 3
    b. 4
    c. 6
    d. 9

7. Lester Hayes played his entire 10-season NFL career with the LA/Oakland Raiders.

    a. True
    b. False

8. How many Pro Bowls was Jack Tatum named to in his 10-season NFL career?

    a. 0
    b. 1

c. 3

d. 5

9. How many Super Bowl championships did George Atkinson win in his 11-season NFL career?

    a. 0

    b. 1

    c. 2

    d. 3

10. What year was Michael Haynes inducted into the Pro Football Hall of Fame?

    a. 1995

    b. 1997

    c. 2000

    d. 2001

11. What year was Willie Brown inducted into the Pro Football Hall of Fame?

    a. 1980

    b. 1981

    c. 1983

    d. 1984

12. Ronnie Lott played his entire 14-season NFL career with the Los Angeles Raiders.

    a. True

    b. False

13. During his 16-season NFL career, Willie Brown played for the Oakland Raiders and which other team?

a. Indianapolis Colts

b. Denver Broncos

c. Cincinnati Bengals

d. Detroit Lions

14. In his 11-season NFL career, Nnamdi Asomugha played for the Oakland Raiders, San Francisco 49ers and which other team?

a. Houston Texans

b. Atlanta Falcons

c. Philadelphia Eagles

d. Arizona Cardinals

15. How many Super Bowl championships did Greg Townsend win during his 13-season NFL career?

a. 0

b. 1

c. 2

d. 3

16. Charles Woodson was drafted by the Oakland Raiders in the 1st round, 4th overall, in 1998.

a. True

b. False

17. How many Pro Bowls was Chester McGlockton named to in his 12-season NFL career?

a. 0

b. 2

c. 4

d. 6

18. How many Super Bowl championships did Richard Seymour win in his 12-season NFL career?

    a. 0

    b. 1

    c. 2

    d. 3

19. What year was Ted Hendricks inducted into the Pro Football Hall of Fame?

    a. 1989

    b. 1990

    c. 1993

    d. 1995

20. Greg Biekert played his entire 11-season NFL career with the LA/Oakland Raiders.

    a. True

    b. False

QUIZ ANSWERS

1. C – 1980
2. A – True
3. B – 9
4. C – 2000
5. D – 4
6. D – 9
7. A – True
8. C – 3
9. B – 1
10. B – 1997
11. D – 1984
12. B – False (Raiders, San Francisco 49ers, and New York Jets)
13. B – Denver Broncos
14. C – Philadelphia Eagles
15. B – 1
16. A – True
17. C – 4
18. D – 3
19. B – 1990
20. B – False (Raiders and Minnesota Vikings)

DID YOU KNOW?

1. Jim Otto spent his entire 15-season NFL career with the Oakland Raiders. He is a member of the Pro Football Hall of Fame, a 12x Pro Bowler, and a 10x All-Pro.

2. Charles Woodson spent 11 years of his NFL career with the Oakland Raiders. He also played for the Green Bay Packers. He is a 9x Pro Bowler, 3x All-Pro, and 1x Super Bowl champion.

3. Howie Long spent his entire 13-season NFL career with the Oakland Raiders. He is a member of the Pro Football Hall of Fame, an 8x Pro Bowler, 2x All-Pro, and 1x Super Bowl champion.

4. Ronnie Lott spent two years of his NFL career with the Los Angeles Raiders. He also played for the San Francisco 49ers and New York Jets. He is a member of the Pro Football Hall of Fame, 10x Pro Bowler, 6x All-Pro, and 4x Super Bowl champion.

5. Greg Townsend spent 12 years of his NFL career with the Los Angeles/Oakland Raiders. He also played for the Philadelphia Eagles. He is a 2x Pro Bowler and 1x Super Bowl champion.

6. Richard Seymour spent four years of his NFL career with the Oakland Raiders. He also played for the New England Patriots. He is a 7x Pro Bowler, 3x All-Pro, and 3x Super Bowl champion.

7. Ted Hendricks spent nine years of his NFL career with the Oakland/Los Angeles Raiders. He also played for the Baltimore Ravens and Green Bay Packers. He is a member of the Pro Football Hall of Fame, 8x Pro Bowler, 4x All-Pro, and 4x Super Bowl champion.

8. Willie Brown spent 12 years of his NFL career with the Oakland Raiders. He also played for the Denver Broncos. He is a member of the Pro Football Hall of Fame, 9x Pro Bowler, 5x All-Pro, and 1x Super Bowl champion.

9. Mike Haynes spent seven years of his NFL career with the Oakland Raiders. He also played for the New England Patriots. He is a member of the Pro Football Hall of Fame, 9x Pro Bowler, 2x All-Pro, and 1x Super Bowl champion.

10. Jack Tatum spent nine years of his NFL career with the Oakland Raiders. He also played for the Houston Oilers. He is a 3x Pro Bowler and 1x Super Bowl champion.

CHAPTER 12:

SPECIAL TEAMS

QUIZ TIME!

1. How many Pro Bowls was Sebastian Janikowski named to in his 18-season NFL career?

    a. 1

    b. 3

    c. 9

    d. 13

2. Sebastian Janikowski played his entire career with the Oakland Raiders.

    a. True

    b. False

3. How many seasons did Jeff Jaeger play for the Los Angeles/Oakland Raiders?

    a. 3

    b. 5

    c. 7

    d. 9

4. During his seven-season NFL career, Marquette King played for the Oakland Raiders and which team?

    a. Los Angeles Rams
    b. Pittsburgh Steelers
    c. Chicago Bears
    d. Denver Broncos

5. What year was Ray Guy inducted into the Pro Football Hall of Fame?

    a. 2012
    b. 2014
    c. 2016
    d. 2018

6. How many NFL teams did former Raider Mike Nugent play for in his 17-season NFL career?

    a. 4
    b. 6
    c. 8
    d. 10

7. Current Raiders kicker Daniel Carlson was drafted by the Minnesota Vikings in 2018.

    a. True
    b. False

8. Where did current Raiders punter A.J. Cole attend college?

    a. North Dakota State
    b. South Dakota State
    c. North Carolina State
    d. South Carolina State

9. Sebastian Janikowski played for the Seattle Seahawks for one season. He played for the Oakland Raiders for how many seasons?

    a. 8

    b. 10

    c. 14

    d. 17

10. How many Pro Bowls was Shane Lechler named to during his 18-season NFL career?

    a. 2

    b. 4

    c. 7

    d. 10

11. In his 18-season NFL career, Shane Lechler played for the Oakland Raiders and the which team?

    a. Dallas Cowboys

    b. Houston Texans

    c. New Orleans Saints

    d. Cincinnati Bengals

12. Jeff Jaeger was drafted by the Cleveland Browns.

    a. True

    b. False

13. How many Super Bowls did Sebastian Janikowski win in his 18-season NFL career?

    a. 0

    b. 1

c. 2

d. 3

14. Fred Steinfort was drafted by the Oakland Raiders in which year?

    a. 1974

    b. 1975

    c. 1976

    d. 1978

15. How many Super Bowl championships did Errol Mann win over the course of his 12-season NFL career?

    a. 0

    b. 1

    c. 2

    d. 3

16. Mike Mercer was never named to a Pro Bowl in his 12-season NFL career.

    a. True

    b. False

17. Jim Breech played one season with the Oakland Raiders and 13 seasons with which team?

    a. Cincinnati Bengals

    b. San Francisco 49ers

    c. Cleveland Browns

    d. New Orleans Saints

18. How many seasons did Gene Mingo play for the Oakland Raiders?

a. 1

b. 2

c. 3

d. 4

19. How many seasons did Errol Mann play for the Oakland Raiders?

a. 2

b. 3

c. 5

d. 6

20. Jeff Jaeger is a member of the Pro Football Hall of Fame.

a. True

b. False

QUIZ ANSWERS

1. A – 1

2. B – False, Raiders and one year with the Seattle Seahawks

3. C – 7

4. D – Denver Broncos

5. B – 2014

6. C – 8 (Raiders, Cincinnati Bengals, New York Jets, Arizona Cardinals, Chicago Bears, Dallas Cowboys, New England Patriots, Tampa Bay Buccaneers)

7. A – True

8. C – North Carolina State

9. D – 17

10. C – 7

11. B – Houston Texans

12. A – True

13. A – 0

14. C – 1976

15. B – 1

16. B – False (1)

17. A – Cincinnati Bengals

18. B – 2

19. B – 3

20. B – False

DID YOU KNOW?

1. Sebastian Janikowski spent 17 years of his NFL career with the Oakland Raiders. He also played for the Seattle Seahawks. He is a 1x Pro Bowler.

2. Jeff Jaeger spent seven years of his NFL career with the Oakland/Los Angeles Raiders. He also played for the Chicago Bears and Cleveland Browns. He is a 1x Pro Bowler and 1x All-Pro.

3. Ray Guy spent his entire NFL career with the Oakland/Los Angeles Raiders. He is a member of the Pro Football Hall of Fame, 7x Pro Bowler, 3x All-Pro, and 3x Super Bowl champion.

4. Shane Lechler spent 13 years of his NFL career with the Oakland Raiders. He also played for the Houston Texans. He is a 7x Pro Bowler and 6x All-Pro.

5. Mike Mercer spent four years of his NFL career with the Oakland Raiders. He also played for the Buffalo Bills, Green Bay Packers, Minnesota Vikings, Kansas City Chiefs, and San Diego Chargers. He is a 1x Pro Bowler.

6. Gene Mingo spent 2 years of his NFL career with the Oakland Raiders. He also played for the Denver Broncos, Miami Dolphins, Pittsburgh Steelers, and Washington Redskins. He is a 1x Pro Bowler.

7. Errol Mann spent 3 years of his NFL career with the

Oakland Raiders. He also played for the Detroit Lions and Green Bay Packers. He is a 1x Super Bowl champion.

8. Kicker Jim Breech spent the first season of his NFL career with the Oakland Raiders, then spent the following 13 years with the Cincinnati Bengals.

9. A.J. Cole is currently a kicker for the Las Vegas Raiders. He has been with the Raiders since 2019.

10. Daniel Carlson is currently a punter for the Las Vegas Raiders. He has been with the Raiders since 2018. He has also played for the Minnesota Vikings.

CHAPTER 13:

SUPER BOWL

QUIZ TIME!

1. How many Super Bowls have the Raiders won?

    a. 0

    b. 1

    c. 2

    d. 3

2. How many AFC Conference championships have the Raiders won (as of the end of the 2019 season)?

    a. 3

    b. 4

    c. 6

    d. 8

3. Which team did the Oakland Raiders face in Super Bowl XI?

    a. Green Bay Packers

    b. New York Giants

    c. Minnesota Vikings

    d. Chicago Bears

4. Which team did the Oakland Raiders face in Super Bowl XV?

   a. Minnesota Vikings
   b. Tampa Bay Buccaneers
   c. New Orleans Saints
   d. Philadelphia Eagles

5. Which team did the Los Angeles Raiders face in Super Bowl XVIII?

   a. Washington Redskins
   b. St. Louis Rams
   c. Arizona Cardinals
   d. Seattle Seahawks

6. Which team did the Oakland Raiders face in Super Bowl XXXVII?

   a. San Francisco 49ers
   b. Tampa Bay Buccaneers
   c. Dallas Cowboys
   d. Carolina Panthers

7. The Raiders have made 19 playoff appearances.

   a. True
   b. False

8. Where was Super Bowl XI played?

   a. Miami Orange Bowl, Miami, Florida
   b. Los Angeles Memorial Coliseum, Los Angeles, California
   c. Louisiana Superdome, New Orleans, Louisiana
   d. Rose Bowl, Pasadena, California

9. Where was Super Bowl XV held?

    a. Rice Stadium, Houston, Texas
    b. Stanford Stadium, Stanford, California
    c. Louisiana Superdome, New Orleans, Louisiana
    d. Pontiac Silverdome, Pontiac, Michigan

10. Where was Super Bowl XVIII held?

    a. Tampa Stadium, Tampa, Florida
    b. Miami Orange Bowl, Miami, Florida
    c. San Diego Jack Murphy Stadium, San Diego, California
    d. Metrodome, Minneapolis, Minnesota

11. Where was Super Bowl XXXVII held?

    a. Alltell Stadium, Jacksonville, Florida
    b. Qualcomm Stadium, San Diego, California
    c. Ford Field, Detroit, Michigan
    d. Sun Devil Stadium, Tempe, Arizona

12. John Madden was the head coach of the Oakland Raiders when they won Super Bowl XI.

    a. True
    b. False

13. Who was the head coach of the Oakland/Los Angeles Raiders when they won Super Bowl XV and XVIII?

    a. John Madden
    b. Art Shell
    c. Tom Flores
    d. Mike Shanahan

14. Who was the head coach of the Oakland Raiders when they lost Super Bowl XXXVII?

   a. Jon Gruden
   b. Bill Callahan
   c. Norv Turner
   d. Jack Del Rio

15. Who played the halftime show at Super Bowl XXXVII?

   a. Shania Twain
   b. No Doubt
   c. Sting
   d. All of the Above

16. Barry Manilow sang the National Anthem before Super Bowl XVIII.

   a. True
   b. False

17. Which former Raiders player was named the Super Bowl XI MVP?

   a. Ken Stabler
   b. Fred Biletnikoff
   c. Cliff Branch
   d. Ray Guy

18. Which former Raiders player was named the Super Bowl XV MVP?

   a. Lester Hayes
   b. Art Shell
   c. Gene Upshaw
   d. Jim Plunkett

19. Which former Raiders player was named the Super Bowl XVIII MVP?

    a. Jim Plunkett
    b. Mike Haynes
    c. Marcus Allen
    d. Greg Townsend

20. The Dixie Chicks sang the National Anthem before Super Bowl XXXVII.

    a. True
    b. False

QUIZ ANSWERS

1. D – 3 (1976, 1980, 1983)

2. B – 4 (1976, 1980, 1983, 2002)

3. C – Minnesota Vikings

4. D – Philadelphia Eagles

5. A – Washington Redskins

6. B – Tampa Bay Buccaneers

7. A – True

8. D – Rose Bowl, Pasadena, California

9. C – Louisiana Superdome, New Orleans, Louisiana

10. A – Tampa Stadium, Tampa, Florida

11. B – Qualcomm Stadium, San Diego, California

12. A – True

13. C – Tom Flores

14. B – Bill Callahan

15. D – All of the above

16. A – True

17. B – Fred Biletnikoff

18. D – Jim Plunkett

19. C – Marcus Allen

20. A – True

DID YOU KNOW?

1. Among wide receivers who have won Super Bowl MVP, Fred Biletnikoff is the only one who did not have 100 receiving yards.

2. With kickoff at 12:30 p.m. PST, Super Bowl XI remains the most recent Super Bowl completed in daylight.

3. Super Bowl XI was the first Super Bowl where the coin toss was held at midfield three minutes before kickoff. Before 1976, the toss was held 30 minutes before kickoff.

4. Super Bowl XV was played at the Louisiana Superdome in New Orleans on January 25, 1981, five days after the Iran hostage crisis ended.

5. In Super Bowl XV, Jim Plunkett was the second Heisman Trophy winner to be named Super Bowl MVP. Roger Staubach was the first, in Super Bowl VI.

6. In Super Bowl XV, the Raiders were led by head coach Tom Flores, the first Hispanic coach to win a Super Bowl.

7. As of 2019, Super Bowl XVIII is the only Super Bowl won by a Los Angeles-based NFL team (the Raiders were based in LA at the time).

8. The broadcast of Super Bowl XVIII was historic because of the famous "1984" television commercial, introducing the Apple Macintosh computer.

9. In Super Bowl XVIII, the Raiders became the first NFL

team to score an offensive, defensive, and special teams touchdown in the same Super Bowl.

10. Super Bowl XXXVII was the first Super Bowl in which the NFL's number one-ranked offense (Raiders) faced the NFL's number one-ranked defense (Buccaneers).

CHAPTER 14:

HEATED RIVALRIES

QUIZ TIME!

1. Which team does NOT play in the AFC West with the Las Vegas Raiders?

    a. Kansas City Chiefs
    b. San Francisco 49ers
    c. Denver Broncos
    d. Los Angeles Chargers

2. The Raiders had a 14-game winning streak against the Denver Broncos from 1965 to 1971.

    a. True
    b. False

3. The Raiders have won three Super Bowls. How many have the San Francisco 49ers won?

    a. 1
    b. 3
    c. 5
    d. 7

4. The Raiders have won three Super Bowls. How many have the Denver Broncos won?

    a. 1
    b. 2
    c. 3
    d. 4

5. The Raiders have won three Super Bowls. How many have the Kansas City Chiefs won?

    a. 0
    b. 1
    c. 2
    d. 3

6. The Raiders have won three Super Bowls. How many do the Los Angeles Chargers have?

    a. 0
    b. 1
    c. 2
    d. 3

7. The Raiders currently have won more AFC West championships than any other team.

    a. True
    b. False

8. The Raiders and Denver Broncos have faced off on *Monday Night Football* how many times, making it the most frequent Monday Night matchup in NFL history?

    a. 15
    b. 19

c. 23

d. 29

9. What was a series between the Oakland Raiders and San Francisco 49ers called before the Raiders moved to Las Vegas?

    a. Bay Area Series

    b. Battle of the Bay Area Boys

    c. Bay Battle

    d. Battle of the Bay

10. The Raiders and which team shared the Los Angeles market for 13 years.

    a. Chargers

    b. Rams

    c. Packers

    d. Cowboys

11. The very first game between the Raiders and Denver Broncos was played in what year?

    a. 1960

    b. 1965

    c. 1970

    d. 1975

12. The Raiders and San Francisco 49ers have never met in the NFL playoffs.

    a. True

    b. False

13. What was the final score of the Raiders' largest victory against the Denver Broncos in a 1967 game?

    a. 49 - 0
    b. 49 – 7
    c. 51 – 0
    d. 51 – 7

14. Which player has NOT played for both the Raiders and the San Francisco 49ers?

    a. Jerry Rice
    b. Marcus Allen
    c. Michael Crabtree
    d. Ronnie Lott

15. Which player has NOT played for both the Raiders and the Denver Broncos?

    a. Willie Brown
    b. Marquette King
    c. Chester McGlockton
    d. Lester Hayes

16. Mike Shanahan was head coach of both the Denver Broncos and Raiders.

    a. True
    b. False

17. Which player has NOT played for both the Raiders and the Kansas City Chiefs?

    a. Rich Gannon
    b. Bo Jackson

c. Marcus Allen

d. Rodney Hudson

18. Al Davis started as an assistant coach for which Raiders' rival before becoming the team's head coach in 1963?

a. Denver Broncos

b. San Francisco 49ers

c. San Diego Chargers

d. Kansas City Chiefs

19. The Seattle Seahawks, Cincinnati Bengals, and Tampa Bay Buccaneers are all former members of the AFC West.

a. True

b. False

20. Every team in the AFC West has made at least one appearance in the Super Bowl.

a. True

b. False

QUIZ ANSWERS

1. B – San Francisco 49ers

2. A – True

3. C – 5

4. C – 3

5. C – 2

6. A – 0

7. A – True (It's a three-way tie between the Raiders, Denver Broncos, and Los Angeles Chargers who all have 15 each.)

8. B – 19

9. D – Battle of the Bay

10. B – Rams

11. A – 1960

12. A – True

13. C – 51 – 0

14. B – Marcus Allen

15. D – Lester Hayes

16. True

17. B – Bo Jackson

18. C – San Diego Chargers

19. A – True

20. A – True

DID YOU KNOW?

1. The Las Vegas Raiders, Denver Broncos, and Los Angeles Chargers are tied for the most AFC West championships with 15 each (as of the end of the 2019 season). The Kansas City Chiefs have won the AFC West 12 times. The Chiefs are the most recent AFC West champions.

2. The AFC West is the oldest division in the NFL based on creation date.

3. At the time of this writing, the Raiders lead their all-time series with the Denver Broncos by 66-54-2.

4. At the time of this writing, the Kansas City Chiefs lead the all-time series with the Raiders by 67-54-2.

5. At the time of this writing, the Raiders lead their all-time series with the Los Angeles Chargers by 66-54-2.

6. At the time of this writing, the Raiders and San Francisco 49ers all-time series is tied at seven games each.

7. The Raiders and San Francisco 49ers met annually in the preseason due to proximity to each other until 2011, when a fight between 49ers and Raiders fans in the parking lot of Candlestick Park escalated into a shooting, prompting the NFL to indefinitely ban all preseason games between the two teams.

8. The Raiders, Denver Broncos, and Kansas City Chiefs all have 22 playoff berths each. The Los Angeles Chargers are not far behind them with 19 playoff berths.

9. The Raiders won four straight division titles from 1967 through 1970, five straight division titles from 1972 through 1976, and three straight division titles from 2000 through 2002.

10. Former Raiders head coach Jack Del Rio was the defensive coordinator for the Denver Broncos before his stint with the Silver and Black.

CHAPTER 15:

THE AWARDS SECTION

QUIZ TIME!

1. Which former Raider won the AP Offensive Player of the Year Award in 1982 and 1985?

    a. Kenny King
    b. Cliff Branch
    c. Ray Guy
    d. Marcus Allen

2. Marcus Allen was named the NFL Offensive Rookie of the Year in 1982.

    a. True
    b. False

3. Which Raiders player won the AP Defensive Player of the Year Award in 1980?

    a. Ted Hendricks
    b. Lester Hayes
    c. Art Shell
    d. Matt Millen

4. Which Raiders player was named the NFL MVP in 1974?

   a. Daryle Lamonica
   b. Ray Guy
   c. Ken Stabler
   d. Cliff Branch

5. Which Raiders player won the Bert Bell Award in 1970?

   a. George Blanda
   b. Ken Stabler
   c. Fred Biletnikoff
   d. Willie Brown

6. Which Raiders player won the Bert Bell Award in 1976?

   a. Errol Mann
   b. Ken Stabler
   c. Jack Tatum
   d. Fred Biletnikoff

7. Rich Gannon won the Bert Bell Award in 2000 AND 2002.

   a. True
   b. False

8. Which former Raiders player won the Walter Payton NFL Man of the Year Award in 1974?

   a. Ken Stabler
   b. Cliff Branch
   c. George Atkinson
   d. George Blanda

9. Which former Raider was named the Super Bowl XI MVP?

    a. Ken Stabler
    b. Fred Biletnikoff
    c. Cliff Branch
    d. Willie Brown

10. Which former Raider was named the Super Bowl XV MVP?

    a. Lester Hayes
    b. Art Shell
    c. Jim Plunkett
    d. Todd Christensen

11. Which former Raider was named the Super Bowl XVIII MVP?

    a. Jim Plunkett
    b. Marcus Allen
    c. Howie Long
    d. Ted Hendricks

12. Charles Woodson was named the 1998 NFL Defensive Rookie of the Year Award winner.

    a. True
    b. False

13. How many times in his career was Rich Gannon named the Pro Bowl MVP?

    a. 0
    b. 1
    c. 2
    d. 3

14. Which former Raider won the 2016 NFL Defensive Player of the Year Award?

    a. Khalil Mack
    b. Reggie Nelson
    c. Karl Joseph
    d. David Amerson

15. Who is the only Raiders player to win the Art Rooney Award for sportsmanship?

    a. Russell Wilson
    b. Marshawn Lynch
    c. Richard Sherman
    d. Charles Woodson

16. Former Raider Khalil Mack was nominated for the ESPN ESPY Best NFL Player Award in 2017 but lost it to Aaron Rodgers, quarterback of the Green Bay Packers.

    a. True
    b. False

17. Which former Raider won the 1980 NFL Comeback Player of the Year Award?

    a. Ray Guy
    b. Cliff Branch
    c. Jim Plunkett
    d. Lester Hayes

18. Which former Raider won the 1982 NFL Comeback Player of the Year Award?

    a. Ted Hendricks
    b. Lyle Alzado

c. Burgess Owens

d. Cliff Branch

19. Which of the following celebrities has NOT hosted the NFL Honors Awards Show (as of the 2019 season)?

a. Alec Baldwin

b. Steve Harvey

c. Seth Meyers

d. Jimmy Fallon

20. No Raiders player has ever won a Bart Starr Award, which is given annually to the NFL player who "best exemplifies outstanding character and leadership in the home, on the field, and in the community."

a. True

b. False

QUIZ ANSWERS

1. D – Marcus Allen

2. A – True

3. B – Lester Hayes

4. C – Ken Stabler

5. A – George Blanda

6. B – Ken Stabler

7. A – True

8. D – George Blanda

9. B – Fred Biletnikoff

10. C – Jim Plunkett

11. B – Marcus Allen

12. A – True

13. C – 2 (2001 & 2002)

14. A – Khalil Mack

15. D – Charles Woodson (2006)

16. A – True

17. C – Jim Plunkett

18. B – Lyle Alzado

19. D – Jimmy Fallon

20. A – True

DID YOU KNOW?

1. Derek Carr was named the Week 8 AFC Offensive Player of the Week in 2016.

2. Gene Upshaw was the 1979 recipient of the Byron "Whizzer" White Man of the Year Award. Nnamdi Asomugha won the award in 2009. So far, they are the only Raiders to win it.

3. Charles Woodson was named the October 2015 AFC Defensive Player of the Month in the final season of his NFL career.

4. The NFL hosts an honors show each year where awards like MVP, Rookie of the Year, and Coach of the Year are given out. The show debuted in Indianapolis in 2012. It is hosted in the city that is hosting the Super Bowl on the network that is carrying that year's championship game.

5. Three Raiders players have been named the NFL's MVP: Ken Stabler (1974), Marcus Allen (1985), and Rich Gannon (2002).

6. George Blanda is the only Raiders player ever to win a Walter Payton NFL Man of the Year Award. He won the honor in 1974.

7. Sebastian Janikowski was named the AFC Special Teams Player of the Month four: September 2001, September 2011, November 2011, and October 2012.

8. Shane Lechler was named the AFC Special Teams Player of the Week four times in his NFL career: Week 12 2000, Week 15 2000, Week 2 2004, and Week 8 2016.

9. While with the Raiders, Ronnie Lott was named the 1991 Week 8 AFC Defensive Player of the Week and the November 1991 AFC Defensive Player of the Month.

10. Bo Jackson was named the 1987 Week 12 AFC Offensive Player of the Week.

CHAPTER 16:

SIN CITY

QUIZ TIME!

1. The largest bronze sculpture in America is housed at which Las Vegas hotel?

    a. Golden Nugget
    b. Caesar's Palace
    c. Bellagio
    d. MGM Grand

2. The Las Vegas Strip is not located within the city limits of Las Vegas.

    a. True
    b. False

3. What is the average number of weddings that take place in Las Vegas every day?

    a. 215
    b. 300
    c. 315
    d. 400

4. The Bellagio Chocolate Fountain is certified by the Guinness Book of World Records as the largest chocolate fountain in the world at how many feet tall?

    a. 17
    b. 27
    c. 37
    d. 47

5. It would take how many years for one person to spend one night in every hotel room in Las Vegas?

    a. 488
    b. 388
    c. 288
    d. 188

6. What is the name of the Las Vegas observation tower that is the tallest freestanding observation tower in America?

    a. Reunion Tower
    b. Space Needle
    c. Tower of the Americas
    d. Stratosphere

7. The Mirage Hotel's golden windows actually got their coloring from real gold dust.

    a. True
    b. False

8. Who performed 837 consecutive sold-out shows at the Las Vegas Hilton?

    a. Elvis Presley
    b. Frank Sinatra

c. Billy Joel

d. Tony Bennett

9. What is the name of Las Vegas' NHL team?

a. Las Vegas Islanders

b. Las Vegas Canucks

c. Las Vegas Golden Knights

d. Las Vegas Sharks

10. Over how many pounds of shrimp are consumed in Las Vegas every day, which is more than in the rest of the United States combined?

a. 50,000

b. 60,000

c. 70,000

d. 80,000

11. What is the name of the Golden Knights' arena?

a. Wells Fargo Center

b. T-Mobile Arena

c. State Farm Arena

d. SAP Center

12. Seattle has a minor-league baseball team called the Las Vegas Aviators.

a. True

b. False

13. Which food chain diner offers spontaneous couples a side of nuptials with their Grand Slams. At $199, the wedding package includes a wedding officiant, use of the diner's

chapel, a pancake wedding cake, a champagne toast, and two breakfasts.

  a. Cracker Barrel
  b. Black Bear Diner
  c. IHOP
  d. Denny's

14. Las Vegas ranks as which largest city in the United States?

  a. 20th
  b. 25th
  c. 30th
  d. 35th

15. Las Vegas translates to what, in Spanish?

  a. The Desert
  b. The Meadows
  c. The Hills
  d. The Mountains

16. The Sphinx at the Luxor Las Vegas is larger than the Egyptian Sphinx of Giza.

  a. True
  b. False

17. The "Welcome to Las Vegas" sign is not even in Las Vegas. It is actually in which city of Nevada?

  a. Henderson
  b. Carson City
  c. Paradise
  d. Reno

18. What is Las Vegas McCarran International Airport's code?

    a. LVM
    b. MCC
    c. VEG
    d. LAS

19. It costs the Luxor Hotel and Casino how much per hour to power their pyramid's powerful light beam?

    a. 41
    b. 51
    c. 61
    d. d.71

20. There is a black book that lists all the people who are banned from setting foot inside any Las Vegas casinos.

    a. True
    b. False

QUIZ ANSWERS

1. D – MGM Grand (Bronze Lion weighing 50 tons)

2. A – True

3. C – 315

4. B – 27

5. C – 288

6. D – Stratosphere

7. A – True

8. A – Elvis Presley

9. C – Las Vegas Golden Knights

10. B – 60,000

11. B – T-Mobile Arena

12. A – True

13. D – Denny's

14. B – 25th

15. B – The Meadows

16. A – True

17. C – Paradise

18. D – LAS

19. B – 51

20. A – True

DID YOU KNOW?

1. The Las Vegas Strip is the brightest place on Earth when viewed from Outer Space.

2. In Las Vegas, there is a heavy equipment playground called "Dig This" where you can drive bulldozers for fun.

3. Las Vegas casinos never use dice with rounded corners.

4. Mobster Bugsy Siegel named The Flamingo casino after his girlfriend, a showgirl with very long legs.

5. Las Vegas is home to 14 of the world's 20 largest hotels.

6. FedEx's CEO Frederick Smith put his last $5,000 into gambling in Las Vegas. While playing blackjack, he won $32,000, thus saving his company, FedEx.

7. Before his passing, Michael Jackson had plans to build a 50-foot moon-walking robot of himself to roam the Las Vegas Strip.

8. Las Vegas is sometimes referred to as the "Ninth Island of Hawaii;" because so many Hawaiians have moved to the city.

9. The Nevada Test Site (NTS), 65 miles north of Las Vegas, was one of the most strategic nuclear weapons test sites in the United States between 1951 and 1992.

10. The Hoover Dam is located about 33 miles away from the Las Vegas Strip. It was originally known as the Boulder Dam but was renamed after President Herbert Hoover in 1947.

CHAPTER 17:

ALLEN

QUIZ TIME!

1. Where was Marcus Allen born?

   a. Detroit, Michigan

   b. Seattle, Washington

   c. Oakland, California

   d. San Diego, California

2. Marcus Allen played his entire career with the Los Angeles Raiders.

   a. True

   b. False

3. Where did Marcus Allen attend college?

   a. San Diego State University

   b. Stanford University

   c. University of Southern California (USC)

   d. UC Berkeley

4. How many seasons did Marcus Allen spend with the Raiders?

    a. 8

    b. 10

    c. 11

    d. 13

5. Marcus Allen's ex-wife, Kathryn Edwards, starred on which reality show?

    a. Survivor

    b. The Real Housewives of Beverly Hills

    c. The Bachelor

    d. Southern Charm

6. How many Super Bowls did Marcus Allen win?

    a. 0

    b. 1

    c. 2

    d. 3

7. Marcus Allen won the 1981 Heisman Trophy.

    a. True

    b. False

8. How many Pro Bowls was Marcus Allen named to?

    a. 2

    b. 3

    c. 6

    d. 7

9. What year was Marcus Allen inducted into the Pro Football Hall of Fame?

   a. 2001
   b. 2003
   c. 2005
   d. 2007

10. Marcus Allen was the NFL MVP, Offensive Player of the Year, and rushing yards leader in which year?

    a. 1983
    b. 1984
    c. 1985
    d. 1986

11. Marcus Allen was drafted by the Oakland Raiders in the which round of the 1982 NFL draft, and at what number overall?

    a. 1st, 15th
    b. 1st, 10th
    c. 2nd, 32nd
    d. 3rd, 65th

12. Marcus Allen was the first NFL player to gain more than 10,000 rushing yards and 5,000 receiving yards during his career.

    a. True
    b. False

13. Marcus Allen was named the NFL Comeback Player of the Year in what year?

a. 1990

b. 1993

c. 1995

d. 1997

14. What uniform number did Marcus Allen wear as a member of the Los Angeles Raiders?

    a. 3

    b. 13

    c. 32

    d. 33

15. How old was Marcus Allen when he made his NFL debut?

    a. 20

    b. 21

    c. 22

    d. 23

16. Marcus Allen was named the MVP of Super Bowl XVIII.

    a. True

    b. False

17. How many times was Marcus Allen named a First-Team All-Pro?

    a. 0

    b. 1

    c. 2

    d. 4

18. What number of Marcus Allen's have the USC Trojans retired?

a. 3

b. 13

c. 32

d. 33

19. How many seasons did Marcus Allen lead the NFL in rushing touchdowns?

    a. 0

    b. 2

    c. 3

    d. 5

20. Marcus Allen was named the NFL Rookie of the Year in 1982.

    a. True

    b. False

QUIZ ANSWERS

1. D – San Diego, California

2. B – False (Raiders and Kansas City Chiefs)

3. C – University of Southern California (USC)

4. C – 11

5. B – The Real Housewives of Beverly Hills

6. B – 1

7. A – True

8. C – 6

9. B – 2003

10. C – 1985

11. B – 1st, 10th

12. A – True

13. B – 1993

14. C – 32

15. C – 22

16. True

17. C – 2

18. D – 33

19. B – 2 (1982 and 1993)

20. A – True

DID YOU KNOW?

1. Marcus Allen the only player to have won the Heisman Trophy, an NCAA national championship, the Super Bowl, and be named NFL MVP and Super Bowl MVP. Allen was inducted into the College Football Hall of Fame in 2000, the Pro Football Hall of Fame in 2003, and the California Sports Hall of Fame in 2007.

2. Marcus Allen married his ex-wife Kathryn at O.J. Simpson's Rockingham estate. In her book, Faye Resnick claimed that Marcus Allen had an affair with Nicole Brown Simpson, O.J.'s ex-wife.

3. Marcus Allen was named a unanimous All-American in 1981. That same year, he was also named the Pac 10 Player of the Year, was given the Walter Camp Award, the Maxwell Award, and the Heisman Trophy.

4. In 1999, Marcus Allen was inducted into the San Diego Hall of Champions Breitbard Hall of Fame.

5. Allen holds the NFL record for the oldest player to score 10+ touchdowns in a season, at 37 years old.

6. Allen attended Abraham Lincoln High School in San Diego, California.

7. He shares the NCAA record for most 200-yard rushing games with Ricky Williams and Ron Dayne. Each did it 12 times.

8. Marcus Allen finished his NFL career with 12,243 rushing yards, 123 rushing touchdowns, and 587 receptions.

9. In his later seasons with the Raiders, Marcus Allen had a rocky relationship with owner Al Davis stemming from a contract dispute; Davis referred to Allen as a "cancer" to the team.

10. In 1999, Marcus Allen was ranked 72nd on *The Sporting News* list of the 100 Greatest Football Players.

CHAPTER 18:

THE GOAT

QUIZ TIME!

1. Where was Jerry Rice born?

    a. San Diego, California

    b. Tucson, Arizona

    c. Starkville, Mississippi

    d. Scranton, Pennsylvania

2. Jerry Rice competed on *Dancing with the Stars* and was runner-up to singer Drew Lachey.

    a. True

    b. False

3. Which of the following teams did Jerry Rice NOT play for in his NFL career?

    a. San Francisco 49ers

    b. Seattle Seahawks

    c. Denver Broncos

    d. San Diego Chargers

4. Where did Jerry Rice attend college?

    a. University of Notre Dame
    b. Mississippi Valley State
    c. University of Alabama
    d. Penn State University

5. How many Pro Bowls was Jerry Rice named to?

    a. 9
    b. 11
    c. 13
    d. 15

6. How many Super Bowls did Jerry Rice win?

    a. 0
    b. 1
    c. 3
    d. 4

7. In his 20 NFL seasons, Jerry Rice missed only 17 regular-season games.

    a. True
    b. False

8. Jerry Rice holds the NFL record for most regular-season games played by a position player with how many games played?

    a. 300
    b. 301
    c. 302
    d. 303

9. How many times was Jerry Rice named a First-Team All-Pro?

    a. 7

    b. 10

    c. 11

    d. 12

10. Jerry Rice was drafted in the 1st round of the 1985 NFL draft, 16th overall, by the which team?

    a. Oakland Raiders

    b. Seattle Seahawks

    c. Denver Broncos

    d. San Francisco 49ers

11. Jerry Rice was inducted into the Pro Football Hall of Fame in what year?

    a. 2009

    b. 2010

    c. 2012

    d. 2014

12. In high school, Jerry Rice played football, track and field, and basketball.

    a. True

    b. False

13. How many times was Jerry Rice named a Second Team All-Pro?

    a. 0

    b. 2

c. 4

d. 5

14. How many times did Jerry Rice lead the NFL in receiving yards?

    a. 4

    b. 5

    c. 6

    d. 7

15. How many times did Jerry Rice lead the NFL in receiving touchdowns?

    a. 4

    b. 5

    c. 6

    d. 7

16. Jerry Rice was inducted into the College Football Hall of Fame on August 12, 2006.

    a. True

    b. False

17. Jerry Rice won the Bert Bell Award, given to the NFL player of the year, in what year?

    a. 1985

    b. 1987

    c. 1988

    d. 1989

18. Jerry Rice holds the NFL record for touchdowns with 208.

    a. True

    b. False

19. Jerry Rice was named the *Sports Illustrated* Player of the Year in what year?

    a. 1985
    b. 1986
    c. 1990
    d. 1995

20. Jerry Rice was a member of the Phi Beta Sigma fraternity at the Delta Phi chapter in college.

    a. True
    b. False

QUIZ ANSWERS

1. C – Starkville, Mississippi

2. A – True

3. D – San Diego Chargers

4. B – Mississippi Valley State

5. C – 13

6. C – 3

7. A – True

8. D – 303

9. B – 10

10. D – San Francisco 49ers

11. B – 2010

12. A – True

13. B – 2 (1991, 2002)

14. C – 6 (1986, 1989, 1990, 1993, 1994, 1995)

15. C – 6 (1986, 1987, 1989, 1990, 1991, 1993)

16. A – True

17. B – 1987

18. A – True

19. B - 1986

20. A – True

DID YOU KNOW?

1. Jerry Rice decided to leave the 49ers and sign with the Raiders once Terrell Owens took over in San Francisco.

2. Jerry Rice has written two books about his life: *Rice* and *Go Long: My Journey Beyond the Game and the Fame*.

3. Jerry Rice and his dog, Nitus, were featured in the *Wii* video game *Jerry Rice & Nitus' Dog Football*, which was released in 2011.

4. Jerry Rice wore No. 80 for every team that he played for in his NFL career. The San Francisco 49ers retired his No. 80 in 2010.

5. Jerry Rice was named to both the NFL 75th and 100th Anniversary All-Time Teams.

6. Jerry Rice was the alumni captain for "Team Rice" in both the 2014 and 2016 Pro Bowls.

7. Jerry Rice was born on October 13, 1962, in Starkville, Mississippi.

8. Jerry Rice was named AP Offensive Player of the Year in 1987 and 1993.

9. Jerry Rice was named the 1988 Super Bowl XXIII MVP.

10. Jerry Rice was named the NFC Offensive Rookie of the Year in 1985.

CONCLUSION

Learn anything new? Now you truly are the ultimate Raider fan! Not only did you learn about the Silver and Black of the modern era, but you also expanded your knowledge back to the early days of the franchise.

You learned about the Raiders' origins and their history. You learned about the history of their uniforms and jersey numbers, you identified some famous quotes, and read some of the craziest nicknames of all time.

You learned more about star quarterback Derek Carr, the legendary Marcus Allen, and the Greatest of All Time, Jerry Rice. You were amazed by Raiders stats and recalled some of the most famous Raiders trades and drafts/draft picks of all time.

You broke down your knowledge by offense, defense, and special teams. You looked back on the Raiders' championships, playoff feats, and the awards that came before, after, and during them. You also learned about the Raiders' fiercest rivalries both within their division and out.

Every team in the NFL has a storied history but the Raiders have one of the most memorable of all. They have won three treasured Lombard Trophies with the backing of their devoted fans. Being the ultimate Raiders fan takes knowledge and a whole lot of patience, which you tested with this book. Whether you knew every answer or were stumped by several questions, you learned some of the most interesting history that the game of football has to offer.

The deep history of the Raiders franchise represents what we all love about the game of football. The heart, the determination, the tough times, and the unexpected moments, plus the players that inspire us and encourage us to do our best because even if you get knocked down, there is always another game and another (Sun)day.

With players like Derek Carr, Josh Jacobs, and Devontae Booker, the future for the Raiders continues to look bright. They have a lot to prove but there is no doubt that this franchise will continue to be one of the most competitive teams in the NFL year after year.

It's a new decade, which means there is a clean slate, ready to continue writing the history of the Las Vegas Raiders. The ultimate Raiders fan cannot wait to see what's to come for their beloved Silver and Black.

Printed in Great Britain
by Amazon

14410555R00092